SURVIVING SUCCESS

Cover Design:
Angela Carrington
www.inspiremediallc.com

Classic Publishing
Dover, Delaware 19904
www.myclassicpublishing.com

SPECIAL EDITION

SURVIVING SUCCESS

CHANGES, CHALLENGES & CHOICES

Charlotte V. M. Ottley

CLASSIC
PUBLISHING
Dover, Delaware

CONTENTS

DEDICATION

This book is dedicated to my parents Edward (deceased) and Delores Merritts. My parents are my inspiration; they shared their "Teflon hearts" without reservation. I also thank them for my inherent sensibilities in business. All that I am and ever hope to be, I owe to God for blessing me with parents who are my friends, my inspiration and guiding stars and who have never, ever forsaken me.

Dear Reader,

At this moment you may find yourself at a crossroads, stressed, unclear or perhaps even afraid about what you should do next. I know these feelings all too well. You are not by yourself, as most successful people feel like this at some point. There is help. This book will assist you in making choices, which are best for you during this time in your life.

Success is not a straight line; it's full of twists and turns. What's important is that you survive it all. I have kissed death in the face three times and still I survived. I have loved and lost many times and yet I look forward to love again. I accrued an asset value of a millionaire, and through changes and circumstance I lost it, won it back and lost it again. And, still I rise.

Have you ever thought you were a "master" and then realized you were still a student? Trust me; it's not an easy revelation to accept. I have learned and I have taught. I have led and I have followed. I have given more than most and received much more in return. I have received the highest honors, and represented some of the greatest people in the country, yet still inconspicuously I move throughout a room, understanding there is so much more to learn.

At some point, life interrupts our plans with unexpected realities that can be difficult to face, let alone overcome. Have you ever felt that way? I have been cared for; and now I am a caregiver. I have been written about and I have written for others. Now, I write to you because your value is immeasurable. Your life is even more precious than gold, diamonds and pearls. In order to survive success you must always remember this.

May my words and experiences be an inspiration and a guide to sustain your stride on this proverbial roller coaster journey, we call success.

Faithfully yours,

Charlotte

FOREWORD

This book by Charlotte VM Ottley is an important contribution toward anyone on the path to success, especially executives. It is a culmination of her knowledge gained through personal and professional experiences that will benefit any aspiring and accomplished person. Charlotte Ottley is clearly experienced with helping people maximize their own potential. She applies boundless energy, spontaneous creativity, unrelenting ingenuity, loyalty and limitless optimism to everything she does.

I can say this objectively because I have watched Charlotte as a media personality, worked with her as my consultant, been her co-worker and became her friend. I have also admired her versatility as a professional working in St. Louis, New York and throughout the country. Whether she was an educator, on-air personality, businesswoman, public speaker, community activist, mentor, public relations director, owner of her business or government representative, she has given her all to everything she has ever done.

We got to know each other four years ago and it seems like all forty years of my life. Although we had only known each other for a few months, we immediately began collaborating on a major cultural center in St. Louis. Her tireless work ethic, professionalism, high energy and ability to bring people together proved successful for that project. Her outreach expanded to work with the City of St. Louis and work in the community with organizations like B.A.S.I.C. (Black Alcohol/Drug Service and Information Center); East St. Louis Chapter of the NAACP; Better Family Life; and, the St. Louis Community Empowerment Foundation.

When you close the cover to this book, you will realize why Charlotte has been so successful and how you can achieve even more by following her advice.

Sincerely,

Michael P. McMillan
License Collector
City of St. Louis

NKYIMKYIM
(pronounced n-chin-chin):

This West African Adinkra Symbol represents adaptability, devotion to service, toughness and ability to withstand hardships.

As you see this symbol throughout the book, make it your affirmation. Be encouraged. Be inspired. Take the initiative to be dynamic and versatile in your quest to survive success.

INTRODUCTION

Surviving Success

Much is written and spoken about achieving the proverbial dream of success. For most, becoming successful is not the challenge - sustaining and surviving it, is. Little is written about how to survive success, once we have achieved "it." Each individual has his or her own definition of success. At some point in our lives, our changes, challenges and choices bring us to points that we question our values and wonder, *"Is today truly the tomorrow I dreamed of yesterday?" And, "Where do I go from here?"* No matter the level of accomplishments or fulfillment from success, the ability to sustain success, still remains very elusive for most people.

Defining Success

How do we define success? For this discussion, we will say that success means to have achieved beyond expectations and against the odds to some level of professional and/or personal accomplishment.

For you, success may mean owning your own business, holding a leadership position on the job, stardom or having the kind of love relationship you have always wanted. For all practical standards, you may already be a "star" in your show. But for many including those with "celebrity status," success just doesn't seem to be enough.

Unfortunately, money, great jobs and good relationships alone do not ensure lasting success. To survive successfully and with longevity, you must be able to handle the pressures of day-to-day challenges, expectations, and unforeseen obstacles.

Don't wait any longer. Now is the time to "get an attitude" for everlasting success. Surviving success means choosing, adjusting your attitude about yourself, your current situations and your desires for the future. Please try employing the proven strategies outlined in this book and let them help you to survive success.

The Lifestyle of Success

Success is a lifestyle that includes an attitude for self-empowerment, a vision to see beyond the obstacles, a commitment to serve and an expectation to excel.

You are your business. Through the lessons learned from my entrepreneurial family and during my career, I have established several values for myself that I believe are inherent in truly successful people. These values, along with strategies and insights, will give you control of your success, firmly place you within your own unique cycle of success and keep you spiraling toward your success over and over again.

You can succeed without failing...you already have! *Surviving Success* tackles many questions about how to maintain and excel beyond the old successes, while offering perspectives for your new future. Learn from your own experiences and failure will no longer be a fear factor. Consider your successes as your road map to pinpoint what you did and over came to become successful in the first place.

You will leap forward into your continued success. Finding success can be easy, taking charge of your success and keeping it on track is often challenging.

Surviving Success will help you meet these challenges head-on with simple guidelines, exercises and candid anecdotes. If you are ready to get an attitude, calculate your own value, work your goals, create your personal marketing plan, broaden your vision and survive success, then throw away the old tools of success, forget your failures and get on the cycle of strategies to survive your success.

Valuable Treasures

Throughout this book I have used gems to symbolically reflect stages of success.

Gold represents your God-given strengths. Gold is who you are inside; your character, which never loses its value. It is demonstrated in your attitudes that I will refer to as *Reflect-A-Tudes©*.

Diamonds represent *Reflect-A-Visions©* for the vision to overcome the many challenges you will face. Similar to phases of human life, a diamond, must go through fire, be chipped and sculpted to show the brilliance that is inherent in its essence.

There is no job, business, or relationship that does not require you to serve others and yourself. You cannot lead, if you cannot serve. Success is founded on the balance of both.

Pearls represent a natural state of completion on the journey to success. This is the priceless value of service needed to sustain your success and relationships with others. Pearls strung together by commonalities reflect beauty and powerful unity. I will refer to pearls when describing *Reflect-A-Business©*.

Stories *"On the Way to Success..."*

Throughout this book are anecdotes from my life. Perhaps my first-hand experiences, especially the changes and challenges, will be insightful for you as you consider and reflect on choices along your own journey.

Ottley-isms

Finally, "Ottley-isms" are conclusions based on my experiences and exposure; they are shared to help you explore your own views and opinions.

Thank you for taking this step to become the best you can be and accepting yourself as the natural gems you were created to become. You have now joined millions of other "extra-ordinary" people who often go un-acclaimed, while successfully weathering storms of changes, challenges and choices. This book is especially designed to empower you. Join me on this journey of discovery. Hope you like roller coasters!

Facing Changes, Challenges and Choices

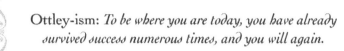

Ottley-ism: *To be where you are today, you have already survived success numerous times, and you will again.*

Dusty Stones

When I was a child I played as a child, danced as a child, loved roller coasters and roller skating, was boldly adventurous, and I loved sincerely and whole heartedly. Now, as an adult, I am grateful that I still do all those things and allow my curiosity and lightheartedness to be part of my world as children do. Too many times adults become stoic, serious and miss the wonders that life brings our way because our hearts are hardened and we have lost our spirit of adventure. *Surviving success* requires an innocence and boldness laced with love to have the confidence to face the many changes, challenges and choices along the way.

I heard a story about a lady who was poor in spirit and only found things in life to complain about. As the story goes, she was sitting on a bench in the park one day, complaining, looking mean and feeling hopeless. A man passed by and without saying anything, gave her a dusty stone. She was angry that it was not money and tucked it away in her pocket and ignored it for quite awhile.

Then one day, for lack of anything better to do, she pulled the dusty stone out of her pocket. She began to rub it with curiosity; and she kept rubbing it with enthusiasm, until it began to shine. Once it began to shine, she became happier, hopeful and each day she looked forward to rubbing it more and more to see how bright she could make it.

One day that same man passed by. She looked happy and not sad. She was very grateful that he had given her the dusty stone and proudly showed him how shiny it was. He smiled and said, I did not just give you a dusty stone. I gave you a diamond in the rough. You used your own talent to make it brilliant, your persistence to get the best shine possible, and your enjoyment to find the beauty. Enjoy your newfound wealth. You became happy even before you knew it was a diamond. You will now reap the value of fulfillment and wealth too. They both must come together for you to be rich.

Do not take for granted how far you have come. Think of your transition as the power of the "pause" which prepares you for an inevitable flow toward even greater fulfillment. We all are given valuable gems. It is what we do with the dusty diamond life throws at us that determine the quality of the life we live.

What dusty stone are you carrying? If you just worked to discover its value, life would be so much better for you. Transitions in our lives give us an excellent opportunity to grow stronger, wiser and more confident than we have ever been. Take this time to find the true wealth within yourself. So, look around because dusty diamonds are always there waiting to be transformed.

ONE

HOW DID I GET HERE?

Ottley-ism: *Be pleasing to yourself in the presence of others.*

Meaning, if you aren't satisfied with yourself it will reflect in how you react to people and how they react to you.

*W*ere you prepared for your last life-altering change? Did it take you by surprise or did you welcome it with open arms? To paraphrase the lyrics of the song, *"Change" "Everything must change. The young become the old. Nothing goes unchanged and nothing, nothing stays the same. There are not many things in life, we can be sure of…"*

Tah-Dah!

A triumphant chord signals the end of a magic trick, as the audience gasps in amazement over the incredible maneuver they have just witnessed. In our own lives, when we have thought of ourselves as most successful, we have received many Tah-Dah's from clients or bosses; friends or family; and even strangers. Too often we lose our footing because we are wholly unprepared for what may follow: job lay-offs, early retirement, our own illness or that of a loved one. So, at some point, our changes, challenges and choices makes us question our values and ask, "Why isn't today the tomorrow I dreamed of yesterday?"

Regardless of the level of your aspirations and the choices you make, this book: *Surviving Success* will help you manage your journey through continuous success. You will learn about the gold that is inherent in God's gift inside of you that never loses its value; your diamond "challenging" experiences that only make you stronger, so your brilliance will always shine, increasing in value; and your pearl experiences that bring the contentment for a life well lived. Discard what isn't relevant to you, save what is and make it uniquely your own as you manage through critical Changes, Challenges &

Choices. It isn't magic at all. It was always you making things happen. So get ready; the stage is set. It's time to start your next Tah Dah!

Challenges Can Create Lack of Fulfillment

Fulfillment from and the ability to sustain success can be elusive personally and professionally. You are not alone. There are no absolutes to success. However, the questions and answers are presented to reinforce and give you options to make better choices. Try these suggestions to help you overcome these challenges.

Challenge #1. Asking for help. This is a tough one. People can't read your mind; you have to ask for what you want. It is a humbling experience when you have to ask for help when you have usually been on the giving end and considered as "successful."

Challenge #2. Learning to accept help, even when it is not in the way you expect. Don't be embarrassed by the generosity of others.

Challenge #3. Handling rejection. Even when you feel humiliated, you have to remember who you are and don't let anything keep you from reaching your goal. Brush it off and keep on striving. You've succeeded before, you can do it again.

Challenge #4. Turning disappointment into your learning curve. When trying something new, be tolerant with yourself. Be encouraged. You've mastered new things, new places, new challenges before; you can and will succeed this time around, as well.

Challenge #5. Practicing being a better listener, and a more astute observer of others.

Challenge #6. Seeing beyond the obvious. Consider the intent and the hearts of others, and yourself, without compromising your integrity to make adjustments for a bigger vision and new experiences.

You are here to continue to survive success. While you are reading this book, you will begin to reassess your skills and to redefine how you can use them to build your "new success" even when you are in the middle of a transition. Some of the same skills, strategies and challenges that brought you to success in the past will be necessary, coupled with your current experiences, to help you achieve what is destined for you today.

TWO

QUESTIONING SUCCESS

Ottley-ism: *Do not make changes just to be accepted by others.*

Often the people you do the most for, appreciate you the least.
Make changes in the best interest of yourself and those who really count.

We all are successful in doing certain things. However, sometimes we get confused or frustrated when the results do not match our expectations. When others react to us differently than what we think we deserve, it's normal to question our worthiness. If you've ever felt this way, you are not alone. Many on the path to success share similar thoughts and feelings, prompting similar questions.

Over the years when helping people in transition in my role as an Executive Coach, I have found that most people have common questions that are frequently asked. Here are ten questions, along with my answers, for you to think about.

1. *Can I succeed without failing?*

Yes, you can. The fear of failure is one of the greatest deterrents for many people. The perception of failure is settling for less than what you are capable of being and allowing it to stifle your desire. There is no failure when you learn from your experience and try again.

Remember, a choice is not a dead end; it's an alternative. If one does not work, try another one. Only you can stop you.

2. *Is it realistic to think that I can make difficult choices, tough out the consequences and come out winning?*

Definitely. Successfully overcoming obstacles is the foundation of success.

3. *Will I ever get to the point when what other people think of me won't bother me?*

No. It will always matter to care about the consequences of your behavior as it affects others.

Find a balance with how others see you and how you really are. Think of others' feedback as a barometer of how you are doing. Always consider the source of the criticism. Everyone does not have your best interest in mind. If you like who you are regardless, let it go. But remember, we all can improve something. Try change because you truly believe in yourself, not only because others do not.

4. *When I know someone has stabbed me in the back, what's wrong with payback?*

Payback has a price. When you confront or hurt others, it always comes at a cost. Do not misunderstand me. There is a big difference between taking a stand for what you believe versus getting even or reacting to pettiness or insecurities. Even better than getting even; is becoming even more successful. Your enemies will either suffer frustration at seeing your success or perhaps even change their minds about you.

5. *How do I respond to temptations when they may compromise my integrity?*

When making choices small or big, be unwavering when it comes to honesty and integrity. Be true to yourself. Being discreet and minding your own business is not an integrity issue, it's a character trait.

6. *Does faith play a role in success?*

Emphatically, yes, faith plays a role in everything you do. In everything you think. Faith and fear cannot occupy the same space. Choose faith, it will never let you down.

7. *Why do friendships seem to change, based on my level of success?*

Remember circumstances challenge many things, even friendships. Along your path to success you will find many new friends. Those closest to you can be instruments of your pain, as well as your gain, but the joy of having them in your life when you do, will remain forever.

8. *Does "fair" even exist anymore in the equation of success, e.g. size, ethnicity, race, age?*

Define what is fair to you in the choices you make. Everything in your life has a "fair" definition. Each person defines what is fair from their own perspective – and theirs may be quite different from yours.

9. *Can I effectively take responsibility for my success and survive the challenges?*

Yes, absolutely without a doubt. Your power is released when your purpose is clear. Focus on the dream or vision, not the distractions of challenges along the way. Don't be afraid of detours. You never know, they may take you to an even better outcome.

10. *Will being good, ever be good enough?*

No. There are as many perceptions of good as those making the judgment call. Plus, successful people are always climbing, even when they are only competing with themselves. Quite frankly, sometimes, it's just not your time; but far more good will be rewarded than not.

THREE

THE CYCLE OF SUCCESS

Ottley-ism: *Success is a continuous cycle.*

*S*uccess starts with believing in yourself and believing you can accomplish something. It involves setting goals, achieving them, and identifying people and opportunities to help you reach them. Proceed with confidence to maximize each opportunity. As you move through the Cycle of Success, you will gain momentum as you productively advance through each stage. As you continue to achieve, it will inspire you to repeat the cycle over and over again.

Success Cycle

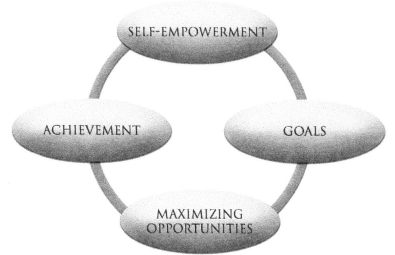

Success is a journey, not a destination. And though you may not reach the goals you expect, review what you learn during the process. Every situation has its own cycle as well. Your job has a cycle, your business has a cycle, each of your relationships have cycles. Every successful person masters one cycle after the other.

You adapt, you continue, and so does the cycle. As long as you realize this, even if you don't achieve at 100% on the first attempt, you can learn the lessons, which will help you succeed through the next phase toward your ultimate success.

Try the cycle with some of your own goals and see how it works for you.

On the Way to Success...
Detours

Even though you set goals, there may be detours along the way that will make you come face to face with changes and challenges, which require you to make tough choices. During the course of my career I set realistic goals, I thought. However, circumstances and opportunities led me in totally different directions than what I had planned.

When I wanted to expand my business, I decided to go to New York to appeal to Percy Sutton, who owned the historic Apollo Theatre. I needed him to help me break into the New York market. I left discouraged because he told me it wouldn't work. He said, "You cannot work New York outside in; you have to be here." Well I had no plans of living in New York. His response was not in my plan.

Before leaving the city, I stopped by WNBC just to visit a friend. While there, he encouraged me to meet his boss. Within 15-minutes of our meeting, she offered me a "job." Well, a job was definitely not in my plan.

I had a dilemma. When I was offered the job, it wasn't clear to me if it was a blessing or a temptation because I really believed I already had what I wanted – I just wanted more of it. I already had a job with CBS. I owned several businesses, and I had personal obligations – all based in St. Louis. I could not tell whether accepting the New York opportunity would take me toward my goal of expanding my business or take me away from my goal by starting something new – namely by going back into the workforce with another job.

Whatever decision I would make obviously meant changes that could bring many challenges, so I had to make choices. It took me eight weeks to make a decision. These were some of my considerations:

Changes: If I took the job, this meant I would have to leave St. Louis. I thought my leaving would mean I was not grateful for what I already had, which was a sure thing.

Challenges: I didn't have the money to make such a jump in living expenses to a big city like New York. And, I would be leaving my support system, including my network and my family.

Choices: I decided to accept the job offer with the understanding that I would continue to manage my network of companies while employed. Once I made the choice, two weeks later, I moved to New York.

Results: I loved New York and it loved me back. In the first year of my transition, my salary was double what I was making in St. Louis with my job and businesses combined. I was welcomed to the New York community at the Rainbow Room, a place that I had admired through television every New Year's Eve while growing up. And, to top it all off, my program won three EMMY Awards the second year there.

I smile because moving to New York had not been in my plan. That's what I call a detour; God made it part of my Cycle of Success. His plan for me was an unexpected, yet welcome blessing far greater than what I had imagined for myself.

Based on my Detour on the way to success, I practiced what I am sharing with you. Apply the Cycle of Success to your own experiences and detours.

Self Belief – Believe that you have the capability. Once you make a choice, be enthusiastic about it and sincerely go after what you want.

Goal Setting – Set a goal and look beyond the obstacles. Something even greater could be on the other side.

Maximize Opportunities – Look for opportunities that will propel you to reach your goals.

Achievement – Celebrate what you have accomplished and continue on the cycle to your success, express your gratitude, and share it with others.

Don't take your journey for granted. Embrace the changes, the challenges, the choices, the detours and the opportunities in your life. Remember, *Success is a continuous cycle.*

Strategy One: Get an Attitude for Success

"If we take people as they are, we make them worse. But if we treat them as if they were what they should be, we make them what they can be."

Johann Wolfgang Von Goethe,
Founder, The Hope School

FOUR

IDENTIFYING STRENGTHS

$\mathcal{G}$old is found free in nature. It's considered the "King of metals." It is a soft metal, yet strong. It is a good conductor of heat and electricity and is unaffected by air and most agents. It gets stronger when added to other properties. It can be beaten to expand and its innate value will not be reduced or lost.

Ottley-ism: *You are gold. You are who you are based on your inherent strengths, which are given to you, by God, through your parent's cellular memory. These traits make you unique in your own right. Identify these inherent strengths or attributes, and minimize your focus on weaknesses so that you can accept or manage them.*

Mining your gold begins with an Attitude. What's Your Attitude? Complete this quick questionnaire and find out.

PR Lab ATTITUDE Profile

Mark (√) by the statement that describes your current attitude and mark (√√) by the statement that describes the attitude you would like to have or need to work on.

1. I believe that situations can improve.   _____

2. I feel enthusiastic and capable of change.   _____

3. I see myself doing many new things.   _____

4. I can generate support for what I need to accomplish.   _____

5. Whenever I put my mind to it, I can improve any situation. _____

6. I can try to change, even though I may feel awkward at first. _____

7. I can find alternatives to my problems, by concentrating

   on how to make a situation work to my advantage. _____

8. I tell myself that I trust my ability to push forward

   against all odds. _____

9. I am grateful for the paths I have chosen and know

   I can make even better decisions in the future. _____

10. I care about the consequences of my behavior as it

    affects others. _____

So now that you have identified your current and desired attitudes, use this profile as a reference in facing challenges and choices with decisions you will have to make as you continue your journey to success.

PR Lab Defining You as "The Product" - Personally and Professionally

Not unlike marketing a product, you have to see *"you"* as the product. Especially during times of transition, it may not be clear to you about who you are. At other times, you may be too modest to articulate your attributes to others. Here are some simple questions to help you determine how to brand and present yourself to others.

What are 3 goals you have today?

When talking about yourself, people listen for what you want to accomplish and how that matches their goals. Sometimes people make the mistake of just saying what they think other people want to hear them say, so they do it to get what they want. This is risky business. If you get a job or a contract that really is not a match for you, you will be miserable and you will make others miserable as well. *Changes, Challenges and Choices will follow based on the decisions which you make today.*

Which of these goals did you have 1 year ago?

Which of these goals do you think you will achieve within the next year?

If you have the same goals today that you had three years ago, is it realistic to think that you will accomplish them in the coming year without facing changes and challenges to make new choices? Though there could be many reasons you have not accomplished the goals, be prepared to ask yourself, "Are these still realistic goals?" and "What am I going to do differently this time to ensure success?"

Challenges are only temporary circumstances that everyone faces. How you get through the challenge is a reflection of your attitudes. They ultimately influence your success.

What are major challenges that prevented you from reaching your goals?

Now that you have identified the challenges, plan how you can overcome them moving forward. The following Self-Awareness exercise will support you in building your strategy.

A Self Awareness Exercise

Think of 3 compliments you receive (regularly - at the work place or among friends) and make a list.

Think about the traits or characteristics you like most about yourself and make a list.

Now, take your time and think of what you have achieved and what have been your most successful accomplishments. List those too.

You have just listed the attributes for your success. Each one of them matters.

Now consider these answers in relation to the goals and challenges you listed before.

Are there matches or were your attributes about your personal life, while your goals were about your professional life?

In your list of accomplishments, did you list life events like motherhood or fatherhood, while your goals were all about your professional life? If so, understand the importance of aligning your personal and professional goals as one. They each influence the other.

The intent of this exercise is for you to determine if you can identify the gaps that may exist between what you are saying and what you are actually doing.

Which of these descriptions about yourself "your gold, your positive assets," can help you address the challenges you cited, so that you can reach your goals?

Make sure that your goals support the skills that you currently have – because when you can link your accomplishments and proof of performance with what you want to accomplish, especially in the long term, your chances of success will increase.

FIVE

REFLECT-A-TUDES

 Ottley-ism: *An opportunity plus self-belief multiplied by vision, purpose and faith equals success.*

Reflect-A-Tudes Allow You to Show Others Who You Are Inside

Reflect-A-Tudes evolved when I was working at KMOX TV (now KMOV) in St. Louis. Celebrities would regularly come into the station to tape PSAs (Public Service Announcements). Though they were passionate and of course, very skilled at what they did professionally day to day, the camera could be very intimidating. When I noticed a pattern of nervousness, I would pull them aside, then ask them questions that would trigger confidence, sincerity, and help them get past anything in the way of their showing their commitment and delivering their best message.

It was amazing how these triggers would get them into a mindset that would help them to get on camera, be more confident and believable in their delivery. Their passion was contagious – and based on what they presented, viewers became engaged as well.

Eventually, I coined these six statements as Reflect-A-Tudes. Throughout the years I have utilized these Reflect-A-Tudes to coach many people at speaking engagements at times when they needed confidence boosters, when they were in doubt, or when they were considering change in their lives. This same approach works during interviews, when networking and in building and maintaining relationships.

Reflect-A-Tudes Begin Inside of You

The attitude you have toward yourself influences how you communicate with yourself and then how you respond to others in situations. When you are faced with a situation that you doubt your ability to succeed, Reflect-A-Tudes help you make choices. *Know that you are Gold.*

Only you know your true inner feelings. You may choose not to reveal them to the public, but remember to be true to yourself. If you lose your biblical "inner man" you can lose your way, as well as your foundation. When you are in such a place, "get an attitude," and recite the Reflect-A-Tudes as an exercise to get back on track to acting on your strengths.

1. Think I Can

God has given you something unique and special and it's something that can never be taken away from you. It's how you apply it that reinforces what you can do versus focusing on what you cannot do.

Too often we think of skill driven attributes as what we can do. What I want you to do is think of something that is unique to you – maybe it's your laugh, maybe it's your thoughtfulness, it may be something even more fundamental that gives you a competitive edge in life that should never be taken for granted. It's something about you that when people think of you, your image is the only one that comes to mind. Get in touch with that.

❖ Have you begun on the path to success and stopped because you didn't believe you could make it? If you don't believe you can, why would anyone else? Figure out what you can do and pursue that.

If you need help, get trained in what you want to do by finding someone who can and will support you.

❖ Even the most experienced people get stage fright. If you know you are prepared based on your firsthand experiences, use those experiences to balance your doubts.

Sometimes we have to let go of good experiences of the past, as well as bad ones to move forward. Each new day deserves your "new" best without constant comparison what was. What is, is. What will be, will be.

Yes, you can just get through it and you win. Do not try to sell something you cannot deliver, yet don't be afraid to confidently try something new.

❖ Activity is not equal to accomplishment. If you don't feel prepared, get prepared if being successful truly matters. Don't allow procrastination to make you stagnate. Sometimes people keep working on being prepared and let opportunities right in their face pass them by.

2. Think Enthusiastically

Only when you enthusiastically believe in something will others believe it. It's the key to salesmanship.

❖ Your enthusiasm is contagious and has the power to inspire others to cry or laugh with you. It makes them believe in you.

❖ Even when tasks on your job are dull or challenging, find something you can do to make them enjoyable. There is no cookie-cutter approach to what interests you personally so, when you are enthusiastic, it will show through - just get in touch with that. Your passion will be reflected in your enthusiasm.

3. Think Sincerely

Even a child or an animal can sniff out an insincere person. If you can be genuine in what you say and how you respond, even if it is sometimes hurtful to the listener, people will learn to trust you and consider you genuine.

❖ Avoid being unduly flattering, unless you really are sincere.

❖ Remember that some people will wait to see if your demonstration of sincerity is real because they may not trust easily.

Even when you disagree with a person, if you really believe they are sincere, you can give them the benefit of the doubt. Sincerity is the foundation of building relationships with others.

4. Think Let's

Nobody wins unless everybody wins – don't wait for people to ask you what's in it for them. Plan your goals with consideration of how others benefit.

❖ People like being a part of something good. Better yet, they like to be given credit for their contributions.

❖ When you include others in sharing your success, you ensure long-term success.

Think about those in your life who can make contributions to reaching your goals and success in ways that would be beneficial to them as well. Sharing the labor and the credit is an excellent strategy.

5. Think I Care

When you genuinely show that you care about yourself, your beliefs, and those you love, it spreads to others. Most people think the opposite is true. I believe if you cannot be right for yourself, you can never be right for someone else.

❖ Show you care in all you do, or don't do it.

❖ Start by treating others the way you would like to be treated. However, be observant and accept that others may need to be treated differently than you do. Caring enough to be flexible will help them to feel comfortable with you.

As your relationship develops, remember that you cannot always expect for "care" to come back in equal measure to you or in the same manner.

How you treat others is your signature and it will impact their lives and memories of you for years to come. Accept each other's differences. Some people need overt attention; for others that would be intrusive. When people need help, it is important to respond in a manner that matters to them. Hopefully, they will be observant and sensitive to your needs and do the same for you someday.

Take a moment and think of three things you care about, and how you have expressed it lately. If there are ways you can improve your expression of caring, try them. You will like how you feel and so will others.

6. Think Proudly

Pride is reflected in your posture, attitude, how you speak, what you do and how you treat and respond to others.

❖ Pride is shown in your environment. Those things you appreciate, you take care of.

❖ Be pleasing to yourself in your alone moments and in your public moments.

❖ Admiring a role model and replicating their attributes can be good; however, feeling inadequate is not. Be a model to others and to yourself. Live up to your own standards and avoid comparing yourself with others.

Pride should not be confused with an attitude of superiority and being egotistical. True pride is behaving and expressing sincere gratitude for your God-given gifts as a symbol or model of your success.

Whenever I tell anyone to think proud, they automatically adjust their posture; so, *"Think proud!"*

Using the Reflect-A-Tudes

Any time you doubt yourself or when you are preparing for an interview, presentation, or an important occasion, you may need an attitude boost. Also, when you start a new relationship and it's important to you to be impressive, remember these tools to get started on the right track. Good relationships don't just happen they are built on these attitudes and on your intentions. Use the Reflect-A-Tudes as you are preparing for your success.

Reflect-A-Tudes©

Think I Can

Think Enthusiastically

Think Sincerely

Think Let's

Think I Care

Think Proudly

Those things we pursue with pride, enthusiasm, caring, a sense of "let's" and sincerity always reinforce the achievements of "I can." You will not fail.

On the Way to Success...

Avoid These Five Actions That Disrupt Success

1. If you have to exaggerate about who you are and what you can do to protect your insecurities, don't do it.

2. If you are confrontational, abrasive and feel the need to show superiority, you will lose the respect of yourself. Don't do it.

3. If you lie or become vindictive and competitive in order to win, you lose your integrity. Don't do it.

4. If you have to compromise your confidence, play down your abilities and lose your sensibilities for others to accept you, don't do it.

5. When you know it's not right and know it won't last, don't do it.

On the Way to Success…Meeting Oprah

We, you and me, have a challenge on our hands as Survivors of Success. Let me tell you why. Recently, I was in the audience of OPRAH's Lifeclass on her network, OWN. Now she is quite an example of *Change Mastery* and living through the cycle of success, which you will read more about in my next book

My revelation came when OPRAH asked the audience of 17,000 people, how many were in pain? By responding on twitter, 77% of the audience said they were. WOW! That only left 23% who felt they had some reconciliation with life; that they were pleasing to themselves; and, for the most part, were happy.

I knew I was on the right track now. The information shared in this book is intended to keep the 23% from falling in the obelisk of the 77% and to reinforce the 23% to stay the course and bring some others with them. There is power in numbers. I feel like an anonymous partner with OPRAH.

Watch out now; we may even bring others with us and start flipping that 77% to a larger number of you who make choices through challenges and find your way to each other before the "pain" of it all draws you into the quick sand of the only reality you feel and know at the time. You never know what the future holds? But you can't stop until you get "enough." Let's continue this journey together.

Let's call ourselves, Change Masters, okay?

Strategy Two: Overcome Challenges

"If you can't fly then run, if you can't run then walk, if you can't walk then crawl, but whatever you do you have to keep moving forward."

Rev. Dr. Martin Luther King, Jr.

SIX

SHARPENING YOUR VISION

Ottley-ism: *Faith in yourself can help you go around, through, and above the challenges that attempt to take you off your path to success.*

A diamond is a natural gem which to the naked eye may be considered of little value because it looks like a stone or rock. But once it goes through fire, is chiseled into shapes and polished to its most brilliant state; it is a most valuable and desirable gem.

The process of refining diamonds is arduous and all successful people have "diamond stages" in life. Therein lies the fate of the diamond. Just like anyone of us seeking to succeed, you will be faced with challenges in attempting to become the "diamond" in reaching your goals. You will be confronted with many challenges that appear out of your control.

Going through losses, intimidation, deception, heartbreak and disenchantment can distract you from your goal and take you off course. But if you recognize these stages as byproducts of success and approach challenges by asking yourself fundamental questions, you will be strengthened by the challenges, rather than defeated by them.

Reflect-A-Visions are triggers to use to question yourself and situations as you are faced with challenges. Asking yourself the questions below, built on using Reflect-A-Tudes from the previous chapter, will help you see through the challenges to make choices which are best for you.

Reflect-A-Vision to Get Through Challenges

By the time you finish reading this book, people around you may wonder why you are talking to yourself as you ponder the numerous questions raised in this book. As you face inevitable challenges, here are a few questions and thoughts for you to consider.

1. Can I see beyond the obstacles?

Yes. Have you ever noticed that every hero in the movies gets through extreme challenges when there seems to be no way out? They always get out and they are always a hero or champion. Give yourself credit; so are you.

❖ Sometimes you need to pause to evaluate or assess the situation and make a conscientious decision whether or not to proceed.

❖ In your daily life practice seeing beyond the obstacles by taking a minute to recognize each challenge as a strengthening exercise for what lies ahead. Be careful of knee-jerk responses to others' agitating behavior. It may prompt you to respond like them and not present yourself from a point of strength. Pause then flow.

2. Can I see the ultimate good?

What makes getting past this obstacle worthwhile? If you can't answer that, then perhaps you shouldn't be heading in that direction at this time.

❖ You may get upset at what appears to be a delay, detour, or obstruction in the direction you are determined to go, however, sometimes what you may perceive as bad, in retrospect, may be a blessing.

❖ Choose to look for the ultimate good and the positive outcome of redirecting your course of action.

3. What are my alternatives?

When faced with a challenge think of all of the different ways you can address it. You can leave it alone and try something else. Wait it out, it's bound to go away. Choose another method, another person, or another time to achieve the desired result. Address it head on and master it. Each of these alternatives has consequences and it's up to you to make the choice.

Give other people the benefit of the doubt and move on if it's not working. When faced with a challenge, consider the pros and cons of each alternative. Sometimes there can be two rights.

For example, someone says you did not call them. You said you did. They checked their message at 9:00 am; you called at 9:04 am. You both were right. People spend too much time disagreeing with others on facts that are irrelevant or don't matter. Don't waste your time on this type of disagreement - particularly in this fast-paced digital age. What truly matters is that you now have a new opportunity to communicate.

4. What is the profitability?

Success often comes through collaboration. If you are motivated by money alone, just remember, all money is not good money. In other words, is it worth your time, your effort and your values?

❖ It's okay to look for how something or someone will benefit you in choices you make. You are valuable and so is your time.

❖ When you think of winning, think of why the win is important, not why you want someone else to lose.

❖ Look for mutually beneficial relationships that are compatible with your values.

❖ If you begrudgingly make sacrifices, you lose even if you achieve your goals. It would be better to cut your losses sooner, than to regret them later.

If you lose, keep your dignity and don't ask for pity. If you win, don't brag or degrade those who have lost. And finally, if you choose to stay the course, then win for yourself and for others as well.

5. What is the potential?

Reflecting a diamond vision and making it through the obstacles against all odds can be extremely difficult. Success is not always quick or tangible. Reflecting your diamond vision is a feeling – and you just know when the potential is there. Today we cannot afford to be frivolous in seeking the potential in every opportunity.

On the Way to Success...
The Plexiglass Ceiling

People talk about a glass ceiling, but a glass ceiling breaks. A plexiglass ceiling doesn't break – it only cracks – and doesn't allow you to get to the other side.

I had a plexiglass experience early in my career in broadcasting, which changed my perspective and made me realize that sometimes being good, just isn't good enough. Also, though we may want something, it may not be meant for us because something better may lie ahead.

Surprisingly, I always thought if you had the credentials and the will, you could get anything you wanted...I still do, by the way. But, my greatest discovery was hitting the plexiglass ceiling.

The company I worked for at the time posted a new job opening for a national position. My experience exceeded every expectation of the job description that included having won my first Emmy. Yet another person with fewer credentials and no broadcast experience was given the position, even to her own surprise.

I was faced with a challenge and choices. The questions I asked myself included:" Do I challenge on the basis of Affirmative Action and choose to sue?" "Do I settle and go back to doing my job, unfulfilled and bitter?" Or, "Do I choose to see the alternatives of how to win in spite of what I thought to be an unjust outcome?"

I chose to remain my job and perform above their expectation. Concurrent to that job, I started my own business, Reflections and Associates. In less than three years I landed a contract that doubled my salary and was able to contribute nearly a million dollars back to communities throughout the nation through initiatives I created for a client. Ultimately my company expanded, with resounding success, to 11 affiliates in different cities - all while maintaining my job.

And by the way, because I chose to stay the course, I ended up becoming president of a national broadcast organization that far exceeded the position that I didn't get initially.

Sometimes you get kicked out on your blessings. It's what you do with a dream deferred that influences your ultimate success. I chose to build on the talents I had (my gold) and I used (my diamond) vision to see beyond the obstacles and found alternatives to succeed.

When you are faced with challenges, use Reflect-A-Visions in making choices to achieve the best outcome for you. Think about challenges you have ahead of you. Use the Reflect-A-Visions as an exercise whenever you have to make a tough decision.

Reflect-A-Visions©

See the Potential
See the Profitability
See Past the Obstacles
See the Alternatives
See the Ultimate Good

Strategy Three: Leverage Your Success

On the Way to Success...
I Failed-Down, But I Kept Getting Up!

We hear the success stories of people who have had major victories over breast cancer, accidents, and abuses. When you are on your way to somewhere and life brings you challenges, it's easy to feel de-railed and dis-couraged.

Throughout my life I had several health challenges that threatened to take me off course and I literally failed-down, but I kept getting up! During high school, I had been President of the National Honor Society and received a four year General Assembly Scholarship. In college, although I partied as much as most and enjoyed every aspect of college life, I continued to be goal-oriented. Instead of vacations I opted for working for the family business and internships.

But my first year of college, while pledging a sorority, my grades dropped. With a "C" average, I had to drop off line. I felt I had disappointed so many people and I was so ashamed. I punished myself.

I realized that this failure was not for me. I returned to school with a vengeance to get back on the Dean's list, which I did. I pledged again with my Big Sisters who were formerly my line sisters and that was humiliating, but I completed what I started and have been a member of Sigma Gamma Rho Sorority for many years.

By my senior year everything seemed to be on track until one day as I was walking across campus, I began having severe abdominal pains - so severe that I thought I was going to die. My mind raced ahead to the many experiences an early death would rob me of: for one, I was still a virgin. Surviving major surgery and a hospitalization, I went on to marry and relinquish my virginity.

I ended up marrying the BMOC (Big Man on Campus). As my husband was at the peak of his career, once again, I experienced a major illness. I lost my job, lost my ability to have children, and only for a minute lost my spirit. Once again I failed-down and got back up. I know it was a national prayer line lead by my cousins one Sunday that brought me back. While in the hospital, I was offered a wonderful position at the University of Missouri-Columbia Medical School. Because I kept getting up, I was able to be successful.

Successful people are able to overcome the big challenges as well as the daily little ones. Sometimes it isn't the big "overcomings," but a lot of little ones that pave the road to your success.

SEVEN

PRODUCING RESULTS

 pearl is a natural gem formed in water, hibernated in a shell to protect it, and formed naturally in its purest state. It represents a state of being that we all seek because it is priceless in its formation and pleasing to those that experience it.

 Ottley-ism: *Claim success in everything you do.*

There is no failure, if you try and then learn from it and use it as a stepping stone for the future.

Putting my priorities in order, taking care of things that matter like my health, well-being and personal success ahead of what I did for others has been difficult for me to do over the years. When I spent all of my time making others happy, putting them first, and making sacrifices, I found myself expecting too much in return. Unfortunately, I learned the consequences of not minding my business the hard way. Can you relate?

Producing Results Means

❖ Take care of your own affairs or someone else will do it for you at your expense.

❖ When you look for trouble, you will always find it.

❖ While you are paying attention to someone else's affairs, yours are being neglected.

❖ Revenge is time-consuming, draining, stressful and has short-term fulfillment.

❖ Be a better listener than talker.

❖ Be accountable by staying on top of your own money matters.

❖ Never put a person in a position to cheat you or lie to you.

Minding your own business has many different meanings, but the bottom line is that you cannot take care of anyone else until you have your business in order. If you think of yourself as the business, and you think of being in the business of success, then what will distinguish you is how well you mind your own business.

Acting out of these principles is demonstrated in the five keys of **Reflect-A-Business** which provide prompts reminding you how to mind your own business. Minding your own business does not preclude charity, compassion and love. It is genuineness of caring, sharing and commitment to others that builds profitable enterprises and strong nations.

However, you must first apply these principles to yourself. With this in mind, use Reflect-A-Business for measuring your success in all you do.

Reflect-A-Business

Key #1 Work to Serve Others

When your attitude, vision and behavior are inspired by the motivation to serve others, your success is apparent and sustaining. So think about how your talents can serve others each time you go into a situation.

Be careful because sometimes your attempt to serve will not be received the way you intend. But it is better to have tried, than to watch a person fail, and say, "I should have offered."

Key #2 Work to Expedite the Mission

You cannot expedite your mission if you don't know what others expect of you and what you can expect of others. Try not to over commit, even though you believe it is attainable. It is better to over deliver, than to raise expectations and under deliver.

Avoid blockers that may take you off of your mission. Blockers come in many forms. You can be your own blocker by getting discouraged, angry, or triggered by others' triviality, greed or jealousy. Other people can be blockers by constantly complaining, or by causing confusion, distractions, temptations, gossiping, by not cooperating, missing deadlines, or by being deceptive.

Stay the course. Get through it. Find your own satisfaction and level of completion. Sometimes negative outcomes happen, even though you have given your best. When these situations occur keep them in perspective, don't lose sight of your goal and remain respectful of yourself and others because your reputation and success are on the line.

Key #3 Work to Excel

Give your best and always think of ways to be exceptional. Sometimes this is risky because you may be inclined not to be satisfied and will have a tendency to do more and more. More is not always better.

Sometimes the end justifies the means. It takes a very strong character to be so confident and clear about your vision.

Key #4 Work to Share

When you share, you are wealthy in your own right. Who you are and what you have is a gift worthy of sharing and you will be the better for it.

Supporting others through cooperative efforts, partnership or simple collaboration and passing on good ideas, good products and good service contributes to everyone's longevity. This increases the chance of your having even greater success.

Key #5 Work to Improve

You want to ensure that your contribution to others is in line with their needs and your capabilities. However, if a process is working don't feel the need to adjust it – in other words, don't fix it, if it's not broken.

If you are ready to get an attitude, to calculate your own value, to broaden your vision, and to survive attacks caused by fear and greed, then throw away the old paradigm of success and failure and get on to the cycle of fulfilling success. Remember that success is a starting point, not an end run and if you do so, you will produce the results you genuinely deserve.

Reflect-A-Business©
Work to Serve
Work to Expedite the Mission
Work to Share
Work to Excel
Work to Improve

Strategy Four: Develop Your Support System

On the Way to Success...
Never Underestimate Your Network

Once I made my decision to accept a position in New York, I had only two weeks to leave. Many dignitaries and friends in St. Louis sent me off with a great deal of fanfare. Before I left a social worker named Sandra Davis said to me, *"I can't give you big things like everyone else, but my former roommate from Howard University lives in New York. I have written her and asked her to meet you and introduce you to some people once you arrive in the city."* I thought this was nice, but meeting her friend was not on the top of my list of things to do. But, I truly appreciated the gesture.

Upon arrival I started my mission to identify the top 20 people I needed to meet to make an impact and reach my goals. A lady by the name of Joyce contacted me numerous times at the request of Sandra Davis to invite me to various events. I was so busy. I always graciously declined and asked her to invite me again sometime. I was on a mission. I had my eye on the prize.

After numerous invitations from Joyce, which I had turned down, she invited me to an event at Gracie Mansion, where the mayor of the city lives. At the encouragement of my secretary who said, "This lady keeps inviting you to events. This time you really ought to go." At the time I was Director of Community Affairs at WNBC. When I learned that a camera crew was going to the event, I thought I'd kill two birds with one stone. I jumped into the news van and rode with them to meet Sandra's friend Joyce.

Once I arrived, the first African American Mayor of New York, David Dinkins, was standing at the door greeting people. With camera crew behind me, I approached the Honorable Mayor Dinkins, shook his hand and introduced myself. "Hello Mayor Dinkins it is an honor to meet you. My name is Charlotte Ottley, I am new to your city. I was invited here tonight by…" and before I could finish my sentence, he turned around and said, *"Honey your little friend is here."*

It turns out that Joyce was Joyce Dinkins, the First Lady of New York. It was on the news that night. Joyce fulfilled her commitment to her former college roommate and friend Sandra. I thank God that she was persistent.

I had been looking for people with titles and positions that I thought would lead me to quick success in New York. Yet, I almost missed real success. My relationship with the Dinkins family not only propelled my professional success, but most importantly, it nurtured me. From the moment I met them I was treated like family.

A similar story happened in NY, when a friend wanted me to meet another person from St. Louis, Georgia Frontiere. We became friends instantly. Months later, I learned that she was the owner of the St. Louis RAMS. We remained close friends. You never know.

I almost messed up by underestimating a referral made by a social worker from my hometown who really cared about me and my well-being. You never know who you will meet along the way, and who may be a key to your success.

EIGHT

STRATEGIC NETWORKING

Ottley-ism: *"Be careful how you live today, for your past will meet you in the future."*

𝒯he least in your network can do the most. Sometimes we are looking so hard, we overlook opportunities right in our face.

Developing Your Personal and Professional Network

People are our most valuable resource. Those you know can provide you with opportunities of all kinds. People can help you to grow your business, start a business, advance your career or even introduce you to a lifelong mate. It's important to recognize contacts which are right in front of you, and to be prepared to offer value in return.

The following exercise will bring to mind those people who have helped you and those you have helped.

1. List those individuals who have helped you.

2. List those you have helped.

3. List those you need to meet to help you reach your goals.

Review your responses.

Answers in #1. Those who have helped you typically include friends and family who offer emotional, spiritual and physical support. Make sure you also have people in this group who can serve as references to open new doors of opportunities. For example, former or current employers, ministers, and community leaders may fall into this category.

Answers in #2. Those you have helped typically include friends, bosses, family and mentees. These are your most valuable testimonials and referrals because they know firsthand, your skill and compassion. They can provide firsthand examples of the results of your contributions.

Answers in #3. Those you need to meet can be difficult to identify or to access. Work to be specific. Find someone who can help you reach your goals like a decision maker or someone in power who can open doors, which may otherwise appear closed. For example, if financial assistance is one of your needs, research funding sources, network at events to meet key people in banking or capital investment and go back to #1 and #2 for referrals.

If there is no one in your current network who can directly make introductions and inroads to people who will help you reach your goal, then you must purposefully target and add new people in your networking efforts. Discard those who are opportunity blockers.

Networking Choices and Consequences

 Ottley-ism: *All networking is not created equal.*

Be thoughtfully selective and alert for unexpected opportunities. Every situation is an opportunity planned or unplanned. When you know what you are looking for, you can more effectively choose your networking objectives. Be prepared and never underestimate anyone. God uses the strangest situations and people to send your biggest opportunities. Networking begins with you.

Pre-Networking Considerations:

What do you bring to the deal or experience?

Who is important to you? Why?

Where can you find the people who can help you reach your goals/vision?

When you find them, what do you want?

What attire and conversation are appropriate for the setting?

If you have been invited for a particular reason, confirm the host's intentions and ask how you should make your approach.

When you are in transition, seeking a change, networking can be disquieting. Though you may have used some of these techniques, it may be awkward when you are going through a transition. So, as you are seeking new opportunities, please consider this list.

Every Situation is a Networking Situation:

 Ottley-ism: *The relationships we create with other people at the beginning can impact the future with them and others for a long time.*

Either they are impressed or turned off. In either situation, they will express their feelings to others. Sometimes it is better to be observant and just go with the flow and let things happen naturally.

Strategy Five:
Consider Choices and Consequences

This success model is presented to help you chart your own strategy for success. Start by identifying a goal and put it at the top of your pyramid. Then work your way from the bottom up to determine whether or not you are doing what is necessary to reach your goals. Incorporate your strengths, your network and your key supporters to help you achieve your success.

With each new goal you can use this model to customize your strategy for personal or professional success. You can adjust this model at any time to keep you on track.

Model for Success

YOUR
SUCCESS

KEY
SUPPORTERS

YOUR NETWORK

PERSONAL & PROFESSIONAL
STRENGTHS/GOALS

NINE

THE TWO SIDES OF SUCCESS

*S*ometimes we are blindsided once we consider ourselves as successful because we don't often realize that there are two sides to success – and it's not always easy. If you are not prepared to face the other side of success, you will not be able to survive it.

Your success is how you define it. If you have read this far, you probably realize that you are the agent of your own success. If you have now accepted that you are gold and you have established an attitude for success; if you have accepted that you can have diamond vision and see through the challenges and past the obstacles; and if, indeed, you know that in order to sustain success, you must work success like a business, then you are prepared to take a sincere look at the duplicity of success – and the other side of trade-offs of success.

Duplicity

With your new perspective on surviving success, look at the examples below. The benefits of success you will clearly understand. It's the trade-offs I want you to consider and be prepared to handle.

Warning Signs: The Other Side of Success

1. When others around you seem to blame their short comings on you.
2. When you feel the harder you work and achieve; the less you are liked.
3. When your standards are raised, those who understand and appreciate them are fewer.
4. When the bigger the gain; the pettier the criticism.
5. When others question how you succeeded.
6. When people ask, "How do you do it?"
7. When people have to dispatch their worst "ill-will;" generate their best "mean;" demonstrate their worst judgment; and spread their worst gossip; then, you know you have arrived.

Any time you notice any of these warning signs, review your own attitude toward success. Use your insight to see beyond the challenges and make choices that will keep you on track.

Below are examples of attitudes and feelings typically associated with success and the other side of success. How well you manage the tradeoffs will determine your ability to survive success.

Success is a Happy Feeling	Trade Off
Enthusiastically striving to reach a goal that you achieve.	Feelings of insecurity, you never had before expressed in statements like, "I did not expect to receive all of this attention and recognition."
Feelings of giddiness and euphoria.	Is it me they are catering to or my money, contacts or position?
Feeling of pride. "Wow! I did it. "	Feeling "I gained a lot to get where I am, but I lost a lot to get where I am, too."
Success is better than you ever imagined.	Thinking "I never knew success would be so demanding."
Being so grateful.	Asking yourself, "What did I get myself into?"

Success is Fulfilling	Trade Off
You feel good inside and out; and it shows.	You can never seem to do enough. The more you do, even more is expected of you.
The world is a happy place and others are happy for you.	You have worked hard for what you have and the pressure never lets up.
You are happy to give everything you can.	Feeling that "No good deed seems to go unpunished."

Success is Power	Trade Off
You are confident in yourself to the point that non-constructive feedback from others will not block your flow to success or break your spirit.	Success in your career does not necessarily mean success in your relationships with others.
You feel you deserve special treatment. You have earned it and feel entitled.	You feel misunderstood and unappreciated by others most of the time.
"Don't they know who you are?"	You become more and more concerned about what others think.
Your standards are high and others need to meet them.	"They" just can't get it right anymore.

Success is Being Talked About	Trade Off
People are excited to meet you.	Other people asking "Who do you think you are?"
Others share stories from back in the old days and many want to work with you now.	People are implying that you must have done "something" to make it this far.
You get perks and invitations to high profile events without even asking.	People think you are a show off.

When situations arise and your feelings of success are being threatened by the trade offs, don't fall victim to duplicity. Claim your victory and survive your success.

TEN

INEVITABLE CHANGES IN LIFE

"Knowing others is intelligence; knowing yourself is true wisdom.
Mastering others is strength; mastering yourself is true power."

Lao-Tzu, Chinese Philosopher

Test your confidence in what you have learned. How would you apply the strengths you previously outlined, the network you acquired, the attitudes, and visions to address the following challenges?

Health Challenges?

People are having heart attacks, strokes and diabetes at a higher rate and younger age than ever in history. Does it come from stress, aspirations to keep up with others, deadly habits, low self-esteem, or a sense of entitlement that makes them feel exempt from all of the warnings? Success is short-lived, if you ignore health challenges. Not only can poor health be fatal to you, but also to others you love. Take care of your health. Do it for yourself. Do it for the ones you love and those who depend on you. But should that health challenge come, have an attitude to face it, the vision to work to survive and even overcome, the humility to accept other's help and the commitment to serve others through it all.

Being a Care-giver for the First Time?

Baby Boomers are discovering at a rapid rate that the tables are now turned and that they have become caregivers to their parents, and in some cases, their spouses. This is a rude awakening in responsibility and role reversals. Reflect-A-Vision and Reflect-A-Business offer paramount survival tools.

Death of a loved one?

An exercise in faith is the only thing I can recommend to get you through this one. Know that if your loved one, loved you, they would only want the best for you. Give it to them and love yourself as they once loved you. Remember those things that fortify you.

Sometimes your loved ones are still alive but challenges have caused you to make choices not to speak or interact with them – which can be the "death of the relationship." If you will have regrets after they are gone, do and say what you need to say while they are alive. You will be the stronger for it and whether they tell you are not, so will they.

Loss of a job or business?

Stay prepared. You may have gotten kicked out to your blessing. Work your networking chart and reevaluate your skills. There is no perfect resume, only perfect timing and preparedness. Build collaborations with others. A percentage of something is better than 100% of nothing.

Hopefully you treated your employees and vendors or clients well. They may be your future employer.

Allegations that tarnish your reputation?

Do not protest too much. Keep being the best you can be. Do not get distracted. Keep your eye on the goal and the gold! Let those who truly know you be your champions. Stand tall based on who you know you are. Shoulder the responsibility, if it is yours to shoulder. Rise above it. Do what is necessary for retribution and move on.

Divorce and Breakups?

There was a time when people told me that they were getting a divorce or breaking-up with someone, and I would say I was sorry. Today, I am silent and wish them well because I realize each person must find his or her own peace of mind. If breaking up brings peace, then that is far better than just staying in a relationship for all of the wrong reasons. You cannot be right for someone else, unless you are right for yourself. However, I do urge you to be long in tolerance and judgment and short in forgiveness. When you leave, leave with the fulfillment that you did all you could do.

Trouble on the job?

Have you heard the statement, if it doesn't fit, don't force it? All jobs are not a perfect fit, but they are a means to an end. But, even so, bring your best attitude, skill and respect to the job. Just make sure you are not the source of your own misery. What ever the source, others can not make you miserable without your cooperation. Choose to be the best you and show it in everything you do. What you do today, is your reference for tomorrow.

On the Way to Success...

Divine Order Made a Home Run

This story is absolutely a true story. A relative introduced me to an author in Delaware because she felt I was becoming discouraged with my experiences and would not complete the book. I spoke to a lady by the name of Dr Janet Trout. She was very pleasant and encouraging, but I did not pursue the relationship.

Fast forward 8 months later, I sent my completed book to her. Janet was rushing out of town and passed the book on to the editor/publisher. Diana, as a courtesy took the book home, read it and called me on a Saturday morning. A time I will always remember.

The first thing Diana said to me was what do you plan to do with this book? She asked me what I liked and didn't like about it. After about 30 minutes of her inquisitive questioning she said, "Charlotte your book touched me and inspired me. I would like to help you make it what you want it to be." Immediately we began discussing working on a companion book. Now I am listening to this stranger talk to me about this book that had been challenging to say the least. I was in awe. We ended the conversation with her saying she had to leave town and would get back to me when she returned.

There's more. I have to tell it like this because you will never guess how it all ended. PERFECT DIVINE ORDER. Diana and her trusted friend and business partner Gina' went to meet Janet in Florida. That evening they were invited to have dinner with the famous National Baseball Hall of Famer Lou Brock and his wife, Rev. Dr. Jacqueline Brock. During conversation, the topic of books obviously became a point of discussion. Diana and Gina had mentioned to the Brocks that they literally consumed the manuscript to a book, inspired beyond words Diana was in great anticipation to work with the author.

Jackie asked who wrote the book. Gina immediately said, oh, I have it with me here in my purse. Gina pulled out the book. Lou and Jackie Brock, my cousin-in-laws, screamed with amazement discovering with confirmations the book was written by me. What was the chance that Gina would have the book in her purse?

Thanks to Lou and Jackie Brock for this Surviving Success Special Edition and the future companion book to rapidly follow.

This is how Divine Order works. Your steps are ordered to lead you to your blessings and successful outcomes.

1. Don't give up on your attitude, vision and faith in well doing.

2. Live a life knowing you are gold, get through the challenging times because being a diamond is eminent.

Your turn!

Take a "power pause" assessment break

Think about situations when Divine Order has played a role in your life.

Think about where you are today on your path to fulfillment.

There are always signs; don't take them for granted. We often miss them because we become distracted with what isn't instead of what is.

ELEVEN

BALANCING
RELATIONSHIPS AND SUCCESS

Ottley-ism: *How could you do me like that? Acknowledges hurt and anger with a potentially long term negative impact that can haunt a relationship to its demise...*

The hot topic of relationships opens up opportunities for lively discussion and debate for both men and women. I could not end this book about surviving success without discussing relationships. Most people have definitive opinions about relationships based on their own experience and exposure.

What happens in relationships and how they are handled does impact your success because clashes can challenge how you feel about yourself and how others feel about you. Depending on the intensity of, and your response to, the relationship, broken relationships can derail your success. You have to have them, but you also have to manage them. I have identified some of the most challenging relationship considerations.

Being Too Good in Personal and Professional Relationships

For some reason, good is associated with "easy" in both personal and professional situations. Many good women are raised to be respectable, well-groomed, worth chasing and a lady in public; a geisha girl in the bedroom; a partner in business; a housekeeper for the castle in every way; and a queen of hearts, while raising children and balancing society's woes.

Women, who have been hurt, often pass on a great deal of skepticism to their children about relationships. In trying to save them from hurt, they risk causing more hurt.

There is a natural exchange between our personal and professional lives. Some women on the job are tougher than the average man as though they have something to prove. Probably, their compassion has gone unrewarded. Do not feel you have anything to prove on the backs of others peoples feelings. Just be the best you can be and feel good about it; not self-righteous about it.

Changes

Successful men and women, when trying to succeed, often choose mates who appear to be easy companions. But with success comes an increased appetite for more and a sense of entitlement that they feel they deserve and can get. Too often, this is followed by neglect and wandering from their companion. Challenges…

Cheating

When a woman is too wild, a man can't get away from her. Even when they try to get to or stay with the "good" one, she even makes life equally miserable and full of guilt and hurt. Choices….

By default, he often ends up with the worst one for himself because she did not give up; or it appears that men claim bragging rights because that person is so "crazy" about them. Challenges…

Relationships need to get back to mutual satisfaction and to filling the gaps. Choices…

Today, both women and men, have similar needs and desires. Most people want someone to come home to who looks good and makes them feel good and worthwhile; someone who makes their home a castle in every way; who can be the parent, the lover, the friend and provider. Choices…Be there for each other.

Making Up

My mother would always say, "Don't go to bed or leave a person angry. You never know what tomorrow will bring." If you make up after being wronged, then let the past go. Do not continuously remind and hold the other hostage to the past. If the behavior that caused the problem keeps happening, revisit your motives for staying together.

Sometimes I feel relationships should have a renewal period like drivers licenses. But then that's another book.

Sometimes pride gets in the way of making up because we are afraid of what others will think. Pretend you are behind closed doors without judgment and follow your heart, mind and soul together.

At some point you will be faced with choices. If you want your relationship to survive success you must decide on what terms you will share.

For example, if you still love your man, and you still want him, then make it work for both of you.

Careful now, don't look for trouble. I promise you, when you look for trouble, no matter what you find, you will interpret it to be the evidence you needed to prove that you were "right."

Here are some things that have worked for me.

My former husband and I came up with a word: Gah'ba du. It may sound silly, but we agreed that whenever the other seemed to be going off the deep end, someone should throw in the towel by saying GAH'BA DU and the other would concede. The word had no real meaning, it was just silly enough to be distracting and bring us back on point. Instead of being so critical of each other, we played charades and would act out what bothered us about the other that week. It worked because we had not lost sight of being friends, then.

My finance, now deceased, and I had a ridiculous argument once. To resolve it, we wrote ten commandments for our relationship, which we both vowed to adhere to when we disagreed. On occasion, we would have a heated discussion and he would get quiet. I asked him what happened and he would say, *"I was trying to think of which of our commandments would work right about now."* Of course that would make us both laugh and ease the tension of the moment.

Telling People Off or Venting

A terrible mistake people make is reciting a list of things they have done for you before they became angry with you. That makes you wonder if they were sincere in the first place. But, it also lets you know, that maybe they need more expression of appreciation than you have shown. Do something for people expecting nothing in return. If you do have expectations, cut your deal clearly upfront and discuss the consequences up front, not later.

That's What Friends Are For

Relationships with friends are priceless. Just like everything else, changes, challenges and the choices we make test friendships. True friends can stand the test of time, distance, changes and more. You may not always be together or agree, but you are there for each other when it counts. Everyone does not express their love in the same way. Share with them, how you need it expressed. It is their choice, if they can do so. Sometimes the biggest demonstration of caring comes from people who would not be on your short list of friends. Friendship cannot be bought, only felt. Be a friend and get satisfaction out of that. What comes back is a bonus.

Money Can't Buy You Love

The root of much discord among friends and family and even how a person assesses their own self-worth comes from having money or not enough money. Transitions that impact money reveal your true character. The more you have, the more others around you feel entitled. The less you have the more others judge you. What you do, when you do and how you do regarding money should be in harmony with who you are. It is better not to do anything than hold it over another person's head or question your own self-worth with regrets afterwards.

You might choose to make an investment, but investments have risks and no guarantees. Give a loan? Only if you can afford to lose it. Many a well-intended loan was lost on the way to payback. Money doesn't love you back, so don't give it more value than it deserves in the big picture of the quality of your life. *But it sure helps!*

Relationships have their own season. Some good; some not so good. I am not in any way trying to trivialize the serious challenges relationships have. But, I do want you to discuss openly, forgive quickly, mind your own business; and take time to pause and flow. Only you know when you have given your all to make it work and when enough is enough. When you decide to cut your losses, be decisive.

On the Way to Success...
Changes Beyond My Successful Control!

We were a threesome my Mother, Daddy and me. I never thought either would precede me. Not in death and not in health. They always kept me going. I took risks. They fortified me. I excelled, they were always there to show they cared about me and their pride in my excelling was secondary. What mattered to them was that I was fine as a result of the success. They were my best friends and my best business partners. The best parents I could have chosen.

My Dad fought a noble fight against cancer. With all my clout, money and contacts I could not save his life. And, believe me I had support from so many people from all walks of life, as well as friends, family and the best doctors. But, I did it long distance. His last wish was that my Mother and I stay together. The thought of living in New York made her sick. Going back to St. Louis, I thought would decrease my opportunities and slow me down. For two years, we tried it our own way in two different cities, until she had that 1 in 1,000 risk from a medicine she was taking and was crippled with rheumatoid arthritis with all the symptoms of lupus, stroke and more. My Mother was a vibrant, independent and attractive woman who had done all the right things to take care of herself and was now stricken with a debilitating disease. This time, I would not be a caregiver long-distance. This time I came home. Change happened. The challenge was met. I made the choice to leave New York.

Now, I am a parent of sorts taking on responsibilities I never had. You see, my mother was the manager of all of our businesses. Now I was managing her business. I thought, "Oh my God. I couldn't ever do 'that' well enough." She stays angry with herself for needing anyone. I stay angry with myself for not being good enough for her, now. Wow what a cycle of inadequacy we both share.

Luther Vandross wrote a song with the lyrics, *"I'd rather have bad times with you than good times with someone else."* I never liked that song, until I discovered it applied to my Mother and me. There is nothing more rewarding, nor purposeful than the life we share today.

I haven't stopped taking care of business. I was hired by an awesome young man, Michael McMillan, who I never would have met had I not come home. Though I only do consultancy and training, now, I found more fulfillment in a job, yes a job, than I have ever had because of his leadership and compassion.

I am still on the journey and every day, my Mother and I find something to be enthusiastic and laugh about. We look for the potential and the ultimate good in all the challenges we face. And, one day at a time, we try to expedite the mission and still get the job done.

Choices? Care giving is my passion; and my career is my tool to do well as long as I can. It's the new baby boomers career. IT IS NOT EASY! I have learned many lessons the hard way.

I have found a commonality when I speak to other caregivers. Here are a few lessons I have learned that may be helpful for first time caregivers:

1. Have the patience that you would want given to you, if you were in need of care.

2. Understand their anger is not always at you; it is mis-directed anger they have with themselves for even needing you and being dependent on others.

3. Don't take it personally when they seem to enjoy everyone more than you. It's easier for them. Sometimes, you remind them of who they want to be, not who at they are today.

4. They will feel entitled to your money and your time (immediately) whenever they want it. *Didn't you expect the same growing up?*

5. Unconditional love conquers all. Do everything now so you will have no regrets later. Today is their today; yesterday and even tomorrow is yours.

Remember, just because a person birthed you does not mean that they are or can be a true parent. They may not know how, don't want to or just can't. When you have been the best child you know to be, stop and look around you. There are many parent-like figures wanting to love you and help you. Let them.

*Strategy Six: Steps to Sustain Your Success
On the Way to S uccess...*

Take it Easy, but Take It!

Ottley-ism: *"Surviving success is not a one
size fits-all experience."*

My grandfather Jesse Swanson's favorite saying with a hearty laugh
and a wave was, *"Take it easy, but take it."* As a child I never quite knew what
it meant, but people always laughed back and said, *"Thanks, Jess."*

As we talk about surviving success, we discover success is not a one
size fits-all experience. Each of us have our own unique way of feeling and
revealing our success, even though heavily influenced by others' perceptions
based on our job level, celebrity status, associations, cars we drive, houses,
clothing, etc.. Nothing comes without a price and success is no different. You
have probably heard the statement that you cannot be right for someone else,
if you are not right for yourself? Well though it may be a cliché it rings true.
The more you achieve the more scrutiny and judgment you will receive. You
are held to a higher standard of expectation.

To reach any level of success, you can expect to be challenged with
temperaments and perceptions that can take you off track. You have the
power of choice when it comes to your attitude.

❖ Successful people are tolerant and choose not to act out just to prove they are "right." You do not have to tell the world your every opinion as if it is the only "right" perspective.

❖ Listen more and talk less. Some things do not require an answer. I once had a patient we called Bear who could only say one phrase, *"Dream on Dreamer, Dream on."* To him, that one phrase seemed to fit all situations.

❖ Yes, work hard. But make time to play.

❖ Take care of yourself, the way you would someone else. Do not put it off. Do it for yourself.

❖ Know when enough is enough. Enjoy what you have, without feeling the pressure to keep competing and climbing to get more. Many powerful people find that they have enough, but those around them push for more so they, too can be included; sadly, at times, to a point of destruction. Take it easy and enjoy your success.

❖ Taking it easy is not settling. Accept that things may not be what you want today. Today may be someone else's day; tomorrow may be yours. Do not begrudge others. Treat them the way you would want to be treated had you received the same rewards.

In other words…

Take it easy, but take it!

TWELVE

EXERCISES IN FAITH

Ottley-ism: *Faith is the common denominator to success. It is an unharnessed energy fueled with a determined vision of wanting it all the right way. Too often, we want to take short-cuts that can also eliminate all we accomplish.*

𝒰nfortunately, too often people win according to some arbitrary standard heralded as a success model. If we lose we feel terrible and blame it on everyone else; but inside, deep inside we really blame ourselves. That's when an exercise in faith comes to the rescue.

Fundamental Exercises in Faith

Each of us is born with inherent strengths that are uniquely our own. Call it conscious, soul, or heart, it is our special gift. When we are true to it, it guides us, strengthens us, and protects us. It's God's presence in all of us. We all have it. Some people just allow it to become jaded with layers of fears, insecurities, obsessions, and greed. All too many times, models of varying successes are rewarded every week in the media, on our jobs, in our businesses, in our homes and in real life. The most devious always seems to be the most popular. The more glamorous and the richest always seem the happiest, but we know that it isn't always the case. If you watch the celebrity tell-all shows, it makes you wonder if having it all is really worth it. Well it is and you can sustain it by exercising your faith.

Chakras are energy points in the body. When moved they release your power. I will share three of them for you to use as physical exercises to strengthen and release the energy of your faith.

Exercise in Faith #1:
Crown Chakra

Hold your head high. It straightens your spine and shows your pride.

Smile with inner joy using all of your facial muscles. It shows your enthusiasm.

Bow your head. It demonstrates sincerity and humility and releases the tension in your spine.

Exercise in Faith #2:
Third Eye Chakra

Open your eyes wide and move them to the extreme in every direction.

See the possibilities for they are unlimited.

See beyond all obstacles and see the profitability and potential of your dreams.

Look around and capture the ultimate good in all you do.

Exercise in Faith #3:
Heart Chakra

Lift and bend from your waist as you work to serve.

Stretch your arms wide to show you care and to embrace others with a sense of sharing and inclusiveness.

Press the palms of your hands together in front of your chest. Close your eyes and exhale. It relaxes you and brings you peace. No wonder it is the gesture of prayer.

Run in place to excel and improve.

Hold on to another person. Pull together back and forth to symbolically share and balance your combined strengths.

Have fun doing these.

What's God Got to Do with It?

If we by our mere nature cry out for God when things really tragic happen to us and those we love, why not shout out whenever you need help along the way to success? And, it will not hurt to cry out in gratitude along the way, as well.

During 9/11 in New York, many a person who proclaimed themselves to not believe in God, boldly cried out His name when they felt helpless and afraid for themselves and others. I am sure the same happened in New Orleans, in Japan during the tsunami and nuclear breakdown, and in Haiti with the earthquake. The good thing about God is that you don't need a crisis to call Him. You just might need a little Divine guidance and intervention when changes, challenges and choices arise.

Remember to stay in the pause when you are uncertain, so you can flow with all the opportunities that lie ahead. Pause and flow with what you know.

"If you have faith the size of a mustard seed,
nothing will be impossible for you."
Matthew 17:30

On the Way to Success...
Extended Family

Years ago, it was more common for families to extend their family by symbolically adopting people and treating them as family. They are beyond friends and give a real sense of family. Look around you. The criteria of extended family is fulfilling a mutual need with a magnetic-like connection that binds you. I have been fortunate to be a part of a community where extended families were common.

I have a sister, Denise, who has been in my life since she was ten years old and brothers, Glen, Garland and Keith who have been in my life since I was ten. I am confident that God sent me to New York to meet my youngest brother, Raymond; I could write another book on that. Whether you are on the giving or the receiving end, extended families shape your life and balance any disappointments from your own. With no real expectations of return, build these relationships on the strength of who you are; not on what your family is not.

Today, it is important to find ways to embrace others, to create a family-feel for others. *You never know what a difference it can make in their lives and yours!*

THIRTEEN

CUSTOMIZING YOUR SURVIVAL KIT

Ottley-ism: *The relationship you have with yourself is the only one that is guaranteed to last; so, do what it takes to make it a good one.*

*B*y having front-of-mind motivational "boosters" that will inspire you, you can pick yourself up and get back in the race toward your goals for personal and professional success.

Be kind and true to yourself and you will always have what you need to get through.

Find the items that matter to you and trigger thoughts that empower you.

Make a list of those items that bring you courage, when you feel doubtful, happiness when sad, and comfort when you feel lonely. Add them to your kit, e.g. quotes, keepsakes, Bible, etc.

Talent Memory Bank

Make a list of your skills and talents that no one can deny you have, not even you. Make a list of the accomplishments you will never forget. Add them to your kit. Update as you make new accomplishments.

Wishing-Well

Make a list of all you hope for in the future. If it's weight loss, put in a photo of how you want to look. If you want an item, add a photo of it, e.g. cars, diamonds, clothes, house, etc.

Create a TRASH List for Those Reactions And Sayings that Hurt.

Just **TRASH IT**. Disregard them. They just don't matter. Keep on moving.

Give Thanks a Lot.

Give God and others thanks that you are blessed enough to have a life to survive. Remember those who helped along the way and let them know.

At times, a byproduct of being successful is knowing too much. If indeed you know so much, then you need to be smart enough to use it to your advantage.

Be Smart Enough to Survive Success

"Nothing in the world is more dangerous than sincere ignorance and conscientious stupidity."
— Rev. Dr. Martin Luther King Jr.

Read these out loud or think of them as affirmations:

❖ I am smart enough to know that no one can accomplish anything by themselves. Even Will Smith in the movie *"I Am Legend,"* had a dog, a mutant and the love of others that kept him striving.

❖ I am smart enough to know that I have more to learn. Some good, some bad…which will make me a better and smarter person.

❖ I am smart enough to know that people have something better to do than talk to me, so I am smart enough to be thankful and say so when people try to help.

❖ I am smart enough to know that older people were my age at one time. If I like what I see now, I want to strive to be like them.

❖ I am smart enough to know the value of knowledge and its rewards, so I will learn everything I can while I can.

❖ I am smart enough to know that being smart is not good enough. I have to be able to BE everything that goes with smart: enthusiastic; caring about others and sharing without asking; using the words "let's" and "we"; taking pride in what I do or do not do when I know it could be unnecessarily hurtful to others; and being sincere in what I say.

❖ I am smart enough to forgive others who may sound rude, angry or like they are talking down to me when giving me advice. I will listen beyond their tones for the message meant for me to hear.

❖ I am smart enough to know that I will not win at everything, but I will not lose because I did not try.

You Never Know What Awaits You

 Ottley-ism: *Live today as though there is no tomorrow, because you never know what tomorrow holds, in a good way.*

There are many goals we work and pray for that do not materialize. However, there are so many more that exceed our every expectation. If we have faith, we will realize that God has a purpose and plan for each of us. We can only be ready to receive when we understand the Gold within us, get through the Diamond challenges and hold on for the Pearl experiences that await us. Allow me to share my Pearl experience with you.

On the Way to Success...
Legacies

My younger cousin, like my other cousins and me had been given every opportunity in life, except he (my younger cousin), had more money and privileges than all of us put together. He was handsome, academically brilliant, charming, charismatic, the "baby," and he fell victim to drugs. This was a paradox to me. I couldn't put my head around this. Naively, I thought only people who were weak and had low morals did drugs. I also felt helpless and did not know where to begin to help my cousin.

Around that time, a meeting that began as a courtesy to a friend changed my life, and a cause became my passion, and commitment to make a difference. Oval Miller, founder of the Black Alcohol/Drug Service and Information Center, Inc. (BASIC), rolled out his genius and enlightening appeal, shared one fact about addiction, its impact, and the role of recovery, one after the other.

I was hooked. From that meeting on, working with BASIC became my obsession because I was committed to interrupting cycles of abuse that were tearing entire families apart and ruining communities. I expected nothing for myself, only what I could do for others. Those ten years of dedicated service were some of the most rewarding times in my life. BASIC continued to thrive and eventually I went on to work with other causes.

Sixteen years later, a miracle happened. I received *the highest honor I had ever been given.* BASIC announced that they would like to dedicate a building and program in my name: The Charlotte Merritts Ottley Transitional Women's Center. It would help women to be transitioned back to their families and communities and to become self-sufficient after successfully going through a recovery program from chemical abuse.

I had literally, written a prayer for prosperity to bring me financial peace of mind. God gave me CMOTWC to help bring women to self-sufficiency. I prayed for healing for my loved ones. God created a program that would heal thousands of loved ones of many people. I prayed for God's choice of a soulmate who would complete me and I him. God gave me lives that would be healed in a program bearing my name who loved what I stood for without even knowing me. I prayed for excellence in everything I do. And, God in his divine wisdom answered my prayers much bigger than I ever could have imagined, so I might continue to touch the lives of His children so that they, too, might have all the things I prayed for. My prayers will multiply to their fullest intent, not just for me, but for others through perpetuity. The power of prayer and the mission of BASIC together, were a priceless reward for me.

You too have many activities, dear to your heart, that are driven by your passion. You have done more than the average person. You may have taken these activities for granted. Keep thriving and keep sharing; it comes back to you in so many ways. These are elements of your legacy. *What will be your legacy? How do you want to be remembered?*

"Do not tire in well doing for you will reap the harvest
of your labors in due season, if you don't give up."
Galatians 6:9

FOURTEEN

TO BE CONTINUED...

Ottley-ism: *It's your time.*

*S*urviving success is ongoing and requires perseverance, in addition to all of the things shared thus far.

As you dust yourself off and shine yourself up, there will still be times when you forget what it took to get you where you are - let alone, where you are destined to be.

Heartwarming Occurrences

You see, writing *Surviving Success*, has not been easy. Since 1998, I have started and stopped on the concept of surviving success. Through the process, the things I have shared with you have been tested, time and again, in my own life...

At some point in our success, we need confirmation to assure us that we are moving in the right direction. Since I have no children, I often use the young people in my life to make sure I stay in touch with what is relevant for today. Some young people get that success is not just about material success and job titles. They know that real success is also about who you are inside.

I think I am the luckiest Aunt Charlotte in the world. Whether it is my Goddaughter, Nicole or my niece Ashleigh, or nephews Imira or Kellon, they keep me sharp. Just I was thinking of how to close the book to make it more relevant to my nieces, nephews, and their peers, Kellon sent me a letter. Kellon McFarlin is a 24-year old college graduate in communications who is a passionate and skilled baseball player with multiple businesses: photography, real estate and a greeting card business. His strategy has always been to create multi-wealth sources. Here is his letter to me and others which he posted on his Facebook page which speaks to the power of legacies.

On the Way to Success...
From the Mouths of Babes:
Written by Kellon McFarlin
Contributing Author

First and foremost this is the REALEST thing I have ever written. I have finally had a breakthrough on the road to achieving my dream of being a Major League Baseball player, by being signed to an Independent Professional team in New Mexico & I feel that I have SOOOOO many people to thank who have done something to help me get to this point, no matter how big or small it was. I LITERALLY had to go through all of my 2400 friends & write their names down to make sure I wouldn't forget to tag anyone who I wanted to see this, & I still feel like I forgot some people. Some of the people I tagged know me very well, some not so much, & some knew me before I even truly knew myself. Some others I tagged because I know that you are going through adversity in your life or because I know that you are in the process of going after your dreams and there are great odds stacked against you. I hope that what I'm about to write can serve as an inspiration to others who won't let naysayers, negative people, and setbacks stop them from going after what they want in life.

We all go through unexpected turns in life; it's just a part of the process. But as I have been learning it's not about what happens in life it's about how you react to it. When life knocks you down, do you get back up, dust yourself off and keep on going? Or, do you go to the corner cry and complain about it and ask life why me? When it comes to me and baseball, I have definitely had my fair share of adversity to say the least. In the past year alone, I have had my hopes so high that I could have chest bumped with GOD in Heaven, and only a week later have them shot down to where I felt like I was getting bear hugged by the DEVIL in Hell. I have had tons of negative opinions thrown my way throughout my playing career from Little League all the way until now.

I rode the bench on many teams from high school through college. I was subjected to everything from racial remarks to statements like, "You are not worth the scholarship money you are receiving." I went to three schools in three years in three different states and in my whole college career; I didn't do anything worth mentioning until my senior year at Chicago State.

I'm sure like many other people who I have tagged in this note, I have spent many days wondering if I was just wasting my time and if I should just give up and be mediocre and blend in for the rest of my life. But believe me for the 10,000 no's that you may get on the road to achieving your dream, that one YES you get will make it all worth it; knowing that you didn't give up.

I believe that life only tests people who want more out of life, because it's easy to give up on your dreams the moment something unexpected happens. I am like many other athletes, who have played through pain, had to transfer schools after false promises were made and who know what it's like to take pain killers before every game; not so that the pain will go away, but so it will just be bearable enough to play, because the pain of not playing will hurt far worse.

But at the end of the day, all I can say is THANK YOU to everyone!! It all is appreciated and will NEVER be forgotten. I have a JOURNEY ahead of me, to say the least, to get to my eventual goal; and I am ready for it.

Go after your dreams with full conviction and don't worry about how it will happen. Just stay positive and have a powerful reason WHY and KNOW it WILL happen. Best of luck...like Zig Ziglar says, "See you at the top!" and "Shoot for the moon, cause even if you miss you'll land amongst the stars," says motivational speaker Les Brown.

Now you see why, I had to share Kellon's letter with you. It isn't just the older adult who experiences the challenge of success. But, hearing it from a young person should motivate us in transition to not lose faith.

On the Way to Success...

From the desk of Gina' L Sweeney

Inspired by exercises in faith

Wide Open Arms greeting to all and breathe deeply.

Char's Surviving Success has touched me!

I have been embraced and re-warmed by the spoon fed effects of Charlotte's talents and passions—both by her script in these pages as well as being privileged to have gotten a chance to know her better on both a personal and professional level.

I believe Char is an anointed writer and makes successors of anyone who gives to themselves through reading her words of growth. You are benefitted from this deep paradox of unmovable growth in her rooted BUT adaptable accelerating success building daily methods of operations.

I have personally found further profitable success in using her specific illustrations. Char's embracing effects of teaching you as the reader—taking literal action in both your mentally active 'reticulater' decisions will both deliver positive and profitable results! I tried it in a challenging business encounter.

Read this book and passionately pass it on...

My background has been a mix as yours has too. I have found that in all of my mainstream careers that I have always wanted to further comfort others as well as myself. This is the humbled mindset of most. In being pursuant and furthering my present position in life, this quick read *Surviving Success* has projected me into the next positive phase of day-to-day; additionally giving to my healthy positive increases both financially and personally.

NKYINKYIM = Versatile and Grounded

Get yours today and apply it to your life in every way!

Gina' L Sweeney

Security
Piano Teacher/ Artist
Professional Networker and business builder
Professional Public Speaker
Real Estate Rentals
Author/Publisher

On your way to success, may God transmit into your hearts and souls the depth of my gratefulness to those named and not named who also own a portion of my being. Foremost, you the reader, thank you for giving me the opportunity to share with you the lessons I have learned. *May they help you chart your course of continued success and make choices you can live with as you face Changes, Challenges and Choices.*

For those of us going through transitions, I am reminded of the lyrics in a song from "The Wiz," when Dorothy, says,

"Suddenly my world's gone and changed its fate; and I still know where I'm going. I have had my mind spun round in space and watching it growing. And oh, if you're listening God, please don't make it hard to know if we should believe the things that we see.

Tell us should we try and stay or should we run away Or will it be better just to let things let them be...Livin' in this brand new world might be a fantasy but its taught me to love and its real, its so real to me. And, I've learned that we must look inside our hearts to find a world full of love like yours and mine..."
"Home" sung by Stephanie Mills, Lyrics by Charles Emanuel Smalls. From the Album: "Gold"

Welcome to the world of Surviving Success. You are not alone in transitions. I hope you found the reinforcement needed to continue to propel your success. Use these strategies in your continued success and share them with others.

Success is yours. Hold on to your *Gold. The best is yet to come.*

To be continued...

OTTLEY-ISMS

Ottley-ism: *Be pleasing to yourself in the presence of others.*

Ottley-ism: *Do not make changes just to be accepted by others.*

Ottley-ism: *Success is a continuous cycle.*

Ottley-ism: *You are gold. You are who you are based on your inherent strengths, which are given to you, by God, through your parent's cellular memory. These traits make you unique in your own right. Identify these inherent strengths or attributes, and minimize your focus on weaknesses so that you can accept or manage them.*

Ottley-ism: *An opportunity plus self-belief multiplied by vision, purpose and faith equals success.*

Ottley-ism: *Faith in yourself can help you go around, through, and above the challenges that attempt to take you off your path to success.*

Ottley-ism: *Claim success in everything you do.*

Ottley-ism: *"Be careful how you live today, for your past will meet you in the future."*

Ottley-ism: *All networking is not created equal.*

Ottley-ism: *The relationships we create with other people at the beginning can impact the future with them and others for a long time.*

Ottley-ism: *How could you do me like that? Acknowledges hurt and anger with a potentially long term negative impact that can haunt a relationship to its demise...*

Ottley-ism: *"Surviving success is not a one size fits-all experience."*

Ottley-ism: *Faith is the common denominator to success. It is an unharnessed energy fueled with a determined vision of wanting it all the right way. Too often, we want to take short-cuts that can also eliminate all we accomplish.*

Ottley-ism: *The relationship you have with yourself is the only one that is guaranteed to last; so, do what it takes to make it a good one.*

Ottley-ism: *Live today as though there is no tomorrow, because you never know what tomorrow holds, in a good way.*

Ottley-ism: *It's your time.*

ABOUT THE AUTHOR
CHARLOTTE VM OTTLEY

Charlotte Ottley has an eclectic career that spans over 30 years as an entrepreneur, educator, and EMMY Award winning media executive. Charlotte has been an on-air talent with CBS- and NBC- owned stations in St. Louis and New York, while concurrently hosting shows on radio and cable stations. Born into a family of entrepreneurs, The Merritts, Ottley ran her own businesses in St. Louis and New York with affiliates in 11 cities. She has represented the nation's top financial corporations during the height of mergers and acquisitions.

Currently, she is the Director of Communications and Special Initiatives for the Office of the License Collector, City of St. Louis, MO. She is formerly the President of the National Broadcast Association of Community Affairs. Ottley has also been distinguished as one of New York's 100 Most Powerful Minority Business Leaders by Crain's New York, along with Who's Who in Black St. Louis; and received two Public Relations Society of America Golden Apple Awards for two consecutive years in New York.

Donald Trump selected Ottley, along with 99 other business leaders to be included in his book, *"Best Advice I Ever Received;"* Rev. Dr. Suzan Johnson Cook included her as a guest author in her book: *"Sister Strength;"* as did Jo Lena Johnson in her book, *"If You Really Want to Be Successful, Get Connected!"* She was editor of Harlem Culture, a magazine highlighting historic cultural and arts institutions in Harlem. Ottley is author of two workbooks: *"20 Minute Personal and Professional Marketing Plan;"* and *"99 Strategies for Marketing Success."* She conducts accompanying interactive workshops and a customized New Directions PR Lab for successful adults in transition. She also created, *"Youth Speak Out Commun-I-Can,"* to build self-esteem and interactive communication skills for youth.

In 2010, the Charlotte Merritts Ottley Transitional Women's Center was founded in her name to serve women in transition from drug and alcohol addiction by Black Alcohol/Drug Service and Information Center (BASIC).

She holds a Masters Degree in Speech Pathology and Audiology from Southern Illinois University, Carbondale, IL and was unanimously selected Alumnae of the Year in 2004 from its School of Communications. Through the National Minority Supplier Development Council, she earned a certificate in Business Management at Northwestern University, the Kellogg School of Business.

SPECIAL THANKS

Delores S. Merritts, my Mother * Gloria Howze * Edward Tyrone Howze * The Merritts Family * The Swansons * Denise AM McFarlin * Raymond P. Lewis * Bernice Wilson * Cynthia Badie Beard * Glen Lowry * Judith Coleman * Judith Pruitt * Garland Marcano * Keith Tyronne Williams * Michael McMillan * Rev. Johnny Scott * The Gaitors * Malik Ahmed * Don Hubbard * Oval Miller * Ruby Dee * Susan Taylor * Jose Ferrer * Malik Yoba * Xernona Clayton * Anita Malthia * Lou and Jacqueline Brock * Fred Young * The Kennedys of KAI Design and Build * Dr. Alford H. Ottley * The Dinkins * Carol Perry * Allan Cohen * Adrianne Gaines * Fred Douglas * Abisola Faison * Rod Martin * Cecilia Foster * Connie Wilson * Brenda Williams * Denise Nix Thompson * Mark Willis * Dr. Eugene Redmond * The Officer Family * Michael O'Hara, Family & Cast of Revelations * James H. McDonald * The Parks Family * Eldora Adkins * Dr. Katie Wright * Dr. Donald Suggs * David Price * Denise Thimes * The Bosman Twins * Phil Young * Bernie Hayes * Jim Gates * Terry Cole * Phil Perry * Frantz Sainte * Imara and Jamila Cannady * Floyd Henderson * Dr. Sir Abdullah Smith Ford * Carol J. Friar * Dr. Lloyd Thompson * Martin Mathews * The Lyons Family * Bill Baldwin * Brown Marks * Kenny James * Ed Myers * Mr. T * Anna Maria Harsford * The Green Family * The Stelle Family * The Nash Family * The Neville Brothers * Al Roker * William Moll * Judy Girard * Julia Shaw *Derek Noel * Ollie Stewart * The National Black Theater Family * Cast of Might Gents * Sorors of Sigma Gamma Rho Sorority * Les Brown * Obba Babatude' * Carol Noel * Employees and Business Partners of CharDeeMerr Enterprises: Reflections & Associates, RACNG and C. Ottley Strategies * City of St. Louis Office of the License Collector * Better Family Life; Black Alcohol/Drug Service and Information Center; Charlotte Merritts Ottley Transitional Women's Center and Alumni; and the St. Louis Community Empowerment Foundation * Michael Williams * Ernestine Rives * The Harringtons * George Curry * U.S. Ambassador Donald McHenry * Lloyd Williams * Charles Creath * Students from Hunter College, Florida A&M/Florida State Universities, University of Missouri Medical School, University of Kansas Medical Center and SIU School of Communications * Jo Lena Johnson * Dr. Dannett Scott * Yvette Holler * Dr. Janet Trout (ABD) * Diana Gillespie * Gina' Sweeney * Angela Carrington * A host of other friends, relatives, celebrities, dignitaries, affiliates and associates who inspire me. *

IN MEMORIAM

Edward Merritts, my Father, and the first and second generations of the Merritts and Swanson Families * Foster "Jet" Warren * Dr. Barbara Ann Teer * Katherine Dunham * Frank Foster * Georgia Frontiere * Ken Newsome * Ossie Davis * Frank Childress * Rev. John Rouse * Rev. John Doggett * Colonel Clifton Gates * State Representative Eddie Washington * Percy Sutton * Sidney Small * Bobby McClure * Oscar Brown, Jr. * Barry White * Butch Lewis * Isaac Hayes * Richard Jackson * Mae Wheeler * Margaret Bush Wilson, Esq. *

VOICES OF APPRECIATION

Faithful Central Bible Church

"C. Ottley garnered the respect, admiration and confidence of our entire staff as she provided internal intelligence, developed external relationships, and served us with problem-solving consultation during the challenging transition period of our early days of ownership (LA Forum). Many benefited from her vast knowledge, experienced wisdom, and sensitive leadership abilities...she is a valued asset to any organization."

Bishop Kenneth C. Ulmer, Ph.D.
Inglewood, California

Denny's

"Our relationship with Charlotte and her team led to a highly successful business partnership with Mrs. Coretta Scott King and the King Center. In another initiative, we reached millions of African American Christians and raised nearly $2 million in a single year through the Re-Ignite the Dream Project for the National Civil Rights Museum. Charlotte oversaw our entire Black Church Initiative on the West Coast resulting in changed attitudes, significant positive impact, improved our brand and image, and raised millions of dollars."

Rachelle C. Hood
Chief Diversity Officer

DuPont

"Your participation as a panelist was truly a breath of fresh air and was the key element to the success of our session. You were tremendous. Thanks so much for your time. This session was the buzz."

Theophilus R. Nix, Jr.
Corporate Counsel, DuPont Legal

"Reading this book was as though Charlotte was sitting next to me. I could hear her voice in every word. Congratulations! I enjoyed it."

Michael Kennedy
President, KAI Design & Build.

"I thought I was going to just read a few pages and ending up reading the entire book. I laughed, I talked out loud and I cried in parts. Congratulations."

LaShone Gibson
Assistant Dean, Global Affairs, St. Louis University

"Charlotte, you have done more than what many people do in a lifetime...finished a book and have a center dedicated in your name. Congratulations. You should be proud, I am for you!

Michael McMillan
License Collector, City of St. Louis

"Congratulations, Sister Ottley. You call this a little book. It may be small in size, but it carries a BIG message for us all. Your spirit shines though."

Malik Ahmed
Founder, President and CEO, Better Family Life Cultural,
Education and Business Center, St. Louis, MO

SURVIVING SUCCESS
CHANGES, CHALLENGES & CHOICES
SPECIAL EDITION

Additional copies of this book, along with other related items are available online; text the number 32020 and type Char in the message box. Order at www.cottleystl.com.

Jewelry:
You can order your own customized NKYIMKYIM jewelry necklace or pendant in gold or silver. You can even add diamonds and pearls.

CDs:
Order your customized CD of your favorite chapter. CD will include reading the chapter with lively examples that are in addition to those in the books dedicated to the person of your choice.

Virtual PR Labs:
Schedule your PRLab for group or individual sessions online or by phone.

Available through Amazon.com and BarnesandNoble.com

For information on quantity discounts or ebooks
Contact Diana Gillespie
Diana@classicpublishing.net

For Speaking engagements or training sessions, contact
Gina@classicpublishing.net

CHANGE MASTERS
- Getting Through the Cycle of Success -

When making a difference, really makes a difference

When one call, leads to all the right calls

When money matters, and time counts

When one name, says it all . . .

C. Ottley Strategies

Change Masters is the companion book to the *Special Edition-Surviving Success Changes, Challenges and Choices*. *Change Masters* guides you through the profiles and experiences of successful people who survived and thrived as they navigated their life changes, challenges and choices through life's cycle of success. Strategies, ottley-isms, self exploratory tools, testimonials and much more will be shared to strengthen and fortify you through the eminent experiences you will have on your journey. Together we will take step by step in charting your customized strategy. Learn how C. Ottley Strategies can work in your everyday life as well as those you care about.

Contact us now to be listed on our waiting list to receive the first copies this Fall 2012.

Here's to discovering your Gold; becoming a Diamond; and enjoying your Pearls! You know what I mean?

To be continued...

Charlotte DVM Ottley

NOTES